Spirit Life

D1452778

Grace Ji-Sun Kim

Spirit Life

Fortress Press
Minneapolis

SPIRIT LIFE

Originally published by Darton, Longman, and Todd
London, UK

Print ISBN: 978-1-5064-8451-8
eBook ISBN: 978-1-5064-8452-5

Cover design: Kristin Miller

Contents

Acknowledgements

IN WRITING *SPIRIT Life* for the *My Theology* series, I reviewed where I have been and envisioned where I am going. It helped me see the trajectory in my theological journey. Finding my theological space and understanding of God as Spirit has been enlightening, enriching, and liberating.

I would like to thank the DLT publisher, David Moloney, who invited me to write for this series and graciously helped me every step of the way. I am proud to be part of this important series with other leading theologians.

Friends have helped me along the way. Mark Koenig offered valuable critiques and suggestions. I am also grateful for my student assistant Emily Carroll for her time and effort editing drafts of this book. In addition, I am indebted to my insightful research assistant Bruce Marold for his critical suggestions and discerning read of the manuscript.

I am grateful to my husband, Perry, and to my extended family who live in other parts of the world, who encouraged me to continue writing. I wrote most of this book during the summer while my two younger children were getting ready to go off to college. Elisabeth was starting her junior year at Cornell University, and Joshua was starting as a freshman at the University of Pittsburgh. My oldest, Theodore, was working in Manhattan. As I wrote this book, Spirit sustained me through the busyness of life, and sustained my children as they were preparing for the next phase of their lives. The Spirit of God renewed me and helped me through.

Introduction

MY THEOLOGICAL JOURNEY began when our family immigrated to Canada from Korea. Along with many other Korean immigrants, we needed resources, friends, and a community, which the church provided along with a place of worship. That is why our family started attending church and converted to Christianity. The Korean church became our extended family where we attended each other's celebrations such as weddings, birthdays, and anniversaries. The Korean church became an important place for learnings and community. As I attended church, I always had a nagging question: 'Who is Jesus?' I wanted to know more and more about this man who was called the son of God. The more I studied at seminary and during my PhD program at the University of St Michael's College of the University of Toronto, the less I knew.

9

As I struggled to discover more, I fell in love with the notion of Sophia Jesus – a feminine dimension of Jesus that helped me overcome the long-embedded sexism that I experienced in the church, community, and home. However, with the rapid rate of immigration, it soon became important for me to live in community with people from around the world.

I recognised the importance of interfaith dialogue as it helps us to welcome the stranger and befriend those who are different from us. In this context, Jesus became problematic as many religions do not accept Jesus as the son of God. This became a barrier to becoming friends and community.

When I began teaching seminary students, I came across Spirit which became a life changing moment. It has helped me become a better Christian and overcome some of the patriarchal notions of Christology and the doctrine of God. This book, *Spirit Life,* shares a bit of the journey of my overcoming racism, sexism, colonialism, white nationalism to a theology of Spirit-Chi.

The study of theology has been steeped in the white male European consciousness for the past 2000 years. As theology today becomes challenged and liberated by the onset of digital innovation and globalisation, it is essential to exhibit the pivotal voices of those who have been relegated to the margins and invisible silos of our society.

Spirit Life shares an Asian American theology which is centered on the Spirit as an avenue to better understand God in our culture and time. The Spirit is present in the Old Testament as *ruach* and in the New Testament as *pneuma*. When theology was prominently German, theologians used the word *geist* to talk about the Spirit. As an Asian American theologian, it is important to retrieve and disseminate Asian words and religious symbols into the mainstream discourse to better the accessibility and global understanding of God today. One important Asian concept is Chi, which is translated as wind, breath, spirit, or energy, much like *ruach, pneuma* and *geist*. Chi is a helpful term to understand God as Spirit, as it conveys the understanding of the presence of God within the world and within us. This is not easily conveyed through the traditional words for Spirit. As such, we can move towards a nondualist world of theology which provides abundant space to everyone, including the marginalised and the subordinated, paving a path towards liberation and radical community.

Chapter one, 'Racism, Sexism and White Christianity', examines how theology is biography and biography is theology. This chapter describes my social location as an immigrant Asian American woman living in a white nationalist context. Chapter two, 'Hybrid Theology', studies the Asian concept of Chi, which is similar to the Christian notion of the Holy Spirit. As theology is never pure but syncretistic and hybrid, a Spirit-Chi pneumatological understanding is helpful to not only Asians and the Asian diaspora but for everyone. The final chapter, 'Spirit-Chi Theology' explores how we seek God's presence in the world and in our lives. As we search for God's presence in the world, a Spirit-Chi understanding of God becomes helpful and liberative. A hybrid theology is helpful as it reminds us that we live in a small world of inter-relationality, intersectionality and inter-dependence. We need to welcome and embrace one another into God's love and into the kin-dom of God.

1

Racism, Sexism and White Christianity

Immigration

MY LIFE TURNED upside down on January 18, 1975, when my mother, older sister, and I boarded a plane in Korea and flew to Toronto, Canada. My father had left a month earlier to find housing and welcome us when we landed in Toronto Pearson Airport. We packed our essentials into two red bags per person and left our extended family and country of birth to live in a faraway country. Our world, way of life, and religion changed. We had no idea what was in store for us, but my young parents viewed immigration as an adventure toward a good and prosperous life in Canada.

Our lives changed dramatically as soon as we landed in Toronto on that bitterly cold January day. My first language, Korean, was neither spoken nor welcomed in this frigid land. Step by painstaking step, I had to learn the English language, adjust to a new culture, and adapt to a different way of living much different than what I knew in Korea. I could no longer sleep over at my grandparents' home or play with my many cousins. Rather, I was isolated with just my immediate family members.

After spending two weeks in Toronto, we moved to London, Ontario, a smaller city about two hours to the west of Toronto. In London, we met other Korean immigrants who lived in small, cheap, cockroach-infested apartments, ironically called *Frontenac*, which was far from the upscale, gorgeous *Le Chateau Frontenac* hotel in Quebec City.

We were among the many Korean immigrant families who ended up in the three, identical *Frontenac* apartment buildings which each had six floors and ten units on each floor. This was known as a transitional living situation before Korean immigrants found a more pleasant place. However, our family lived in that apartment from my kindergarten year until I was in eighth grade. I shared a small, dingy room with my sister for nine years, which was not easy, but we had no choice.

Some may think that a five-year-old child can adjust quickly to a new country, that I could become a 'Canadian' overnight. This was not the case for me or my family. Immigration took a toll on me, from struggling to learn English, adjusting to the cold climate, and getting used to white people all around me who did not quite understand who I was. It was a difficult adjustment that our tiny family had to make, and it became difficult for my parents to learn English and live in a culture that did not welcome us.

My parents often felt like 'children' trying to communicate with gestures, facial expressions, and smiles. It became grueling for my mother as she just could not learn enough English to hold a steady conversation. She also had difficulties acclimating to the frigid winters and longed for her homeland and to be with her own parents and siblings.

Church

While we lived in those apartments, a young Korean immigrant couple, Mr and Mrs Kim, invited us to church and drove my sister and I there every Sunday. We liked attending church as we were able to make new friends with Korean immigrant kids our age. A year after my sister and I went to church, my parents started attending, perhaps out of boredom or curiosity. But once they started, they got 'hooked' on church, attended every Sunday, and stayed all day long. On a typical Sunday, our family went to worship, then to Bible study group, and then to a church member's home to eat dinner. I enjoyed having dinner at different church members' homes as it reminded me of the fun that I had with my cousins back in Korea. I couldn't wait until Sunday nights to play with my Korean church friends. My parents went to Wednesday night Bible study, then to Friday night church gatherings, and to early morning prayer meetings on Sundays at 6 am. The church eventually became our extended family as we celebrated birthdays and anniversaries together as if we were one big family. The church was the center of life for the immigrant community. We told our hometown stories, shared Korean recipes, and cooked Korean food together. During these celebrations, I missed my large family back in Korea.

Eventually church consumed our lives. My dad drove my sister and me to various white Anglo English speaking churches around London, Ontario. My parents probably thought it was both free babysitting services and free English classes. Hence, my dad drove us to Missionary Alliance Church on Friday nights for games and fellowship, Sunday mornings to a Baptist Church for Sunday school, and a different smaller Baptist Church on Sunday evenings for worship. As a family we attended the Korean Presbyterian Church in the afternoons. Many of the Korean immigrant churches rented churches from a white church and hence had to hold worship in the afternoons after the white church finished their worship service. Every week was a busy church week for our family. For our small family, there was no way of being and living without the church. These early church experiences impacted my Christianity and theology as it was very conservative. Conservative Christian practices and teachings were the norm in my childhood, and it was only later in my adulthood that I began to challenge and deconstruct white Christianity which was so ingrained in my childhood.

School Life and Racism

I was placed in kindergarten in the middle of the school year in February 1975 without any knowledge of English. As a child who couldn't speak English or understand it, going to school proved very difficult. I was constantly made fun of due to my Asian features. This mocking of my Asian difference was difficult to endure as I had never experienced it in Korea. Racism, discrimination, and marginalisation put a stain on people's lives. It is harsh to endure. Racism is painful. It diminishes one's spirits and forces one to face daily discrimination during recess and in the classroom.

When kids call you derogatory names such as 'Jap' or 'Chink' it is painful. When kids insist that there is no such thing as a Korean, it damages your soul and well-being. That is exactly how I felt daily being called derogatory names and hearing '*ching-chong*' yelled to my face. As I recall such terrible memories, how do I overcome and become the full being that God has created me to be?

Facing racism daily made my childhood years an overwhelming time. It was difficult to overcome some of the trials and difficulties of daily discrimination, racism, and xenophobia which I faced as an immigrant child growing up in the small white city of London, Ontario. Racism wears down one's soul. It breaks one down and it becomes difficult to resist the problems it creates.

I did not have the language or the courage to fight back against the racism, which was present in the school yard, on the streets, and in the apartment building where I lived. I felt like a punching bag for white kids to make fun of and taunt. I felt powerless. They all thought it was a big joke to make fun of me and the other immigrant kids. But racism hurts, destroys our being, and breaks down the soul. We must try our best to resist and recover from the destructive powers of racism. This is not accomplished overnight. It takes tremendous effort to dismantle white supremacy, fight discrimination, and end marginalisation. Fighting racism and discrimination needs to happen in society, schools, workplaces, and churches. So much racism is embedded in culture and Christianity. Therefore, it becomes crucial to disrupt it in our theology and church doctrines. A dominant white Christianity does injustice to the world which is not white.

White Christianity

I grew up with white Christianity and did not know any other forms of Christianity could exist. White Christianity was taught to me at my Korean Presbyterian church as well as all the extraneous churches that my dad drove my sister and I to attend throughout the week. White Christianity is what I breathed and believed; it painted a white God and a white Jesus. We even had the classic *Head of Christ* image by Warner Sallman in our living room throughout my childhood and teens. The consequences of a white God and a white Jesus is that white people then believe they are better than people of color as their whiteness puts them closer to God.

Whiteness is a cultural, political, and religious aspect of North America, Europe, and much of the world, which presents a hierarchy of people according to their skin color with the darkest being at the bottom. Whiteness looks at people of color and accuses them of cutting in line to receive unearned entitlements which white people receive without question. The few whites at the top who benefit from the status quo offer those relegated to the underside as scapegoats to distract us.[1] The anger of people of color over their predicament and mistreatment is misdirected as they should direct their anger against those who are benefiting from the status quo rather than against those who share their economic plight. The status quo of whites holding and maintaining power needs to be challenged

[1]   Miguel De LaTorre, *Decolonizing Christianity: Becoming Bad Ass Believers* (Grand Rapids: Eerdmans, 2021), 96.

and dismantled, as it only serves whites and marginalises people of color.

Whites promote a white Christianity, which has negative effects on people of color. White Christianity came from white male Eurocentric theologians and is the dominant form of Christianity around the world. It emerged during the Greco-Roman period, it is maintained by white male European theologians, and it was spread throughout the world by white missionaries. White Christianity views and presents Jesus as a white male European Lord and Savior. God is understood as an old white male sitting on a throne up in the sky. This is the dominant view of Christianity today as white Christianity is shared and spread throughout the world.

White European missionaries spread white Christianity through the world where it was adopted by Africans, Asians, South Americans, and people in every place where the good news was spread. This form of Christianity maintained itself as the 'true' Christian faith and told the rest of the world to admire white people, culture, history, and identity. As white Christianity spread, it created distorted identities and perceptions of people of color around the globe. People of color were told that the standard of greatness and personhood was 'white' and thus people of color needed to strive to become like them and be less 'barbaric', less 'uneducated', less 'superstitious', and less 'ethnic and cultural'.

White European Christianity promotes racism and superiority of whites above people of color. White Christianity damages society and culture as it marginalises people of color. It also diminishes Christianity which is about love, grace, mercy, and liberation rather than domination and power. Whiteness tends to view foreigners with suspicion and tends to blame them whenever any troubles arise. Foreigners are often accused of taking jobs, opportunities, and even college places away from whites. White Christianity allowed a genocide against the Native Americans and enforced the enslavement of Africans. White Christianity created a fear of Mexicans and enforced the Chinese Exclusion Act of 1882. White Christianity continues to uplift 'whiteness' and push down people of color. White Christianity is often tied to white supremacy, which is home grown and sprouted from American soil. Genocide was made possible by white politics, which promoted whiteness as the human standard. This white politics established the inferiority of people of color[2] in comparison to white people. We must reject white supremacy, which is linked to white Christianity, as it is immoral and hurtful to people of color. We need to create a more equal and just world where all are treated equally.

White classism reinforced by capitalism creates a way of life that is critical to most whites.[3] White people believe that people of color are lazy and want hand-outs from the government. White caste continues to

[2] Miguel De LaTorre, *Decolonizing Christianity: Becoming Bad Ass Believers* (Grand Rapids: Eerdmans, 2021), 150.
[3] Miguel De LaTorre, *Decolonizing Christianity: Becoming Bad Ass Believers* (Grand Rapids: Eerdmans, 2021), 38.

uphold whites as a standard that people of color should strive for. White preachers told Asians we were less than at every opportunity, and white missionaries had to convert heathens to Christianity. How can Christianity allow racism, discrimination, xenophobia, colonialism, and enslavement to occur? Christianity needs to be the good news that all people are created equal and freed to work for justice and liberation of all oppressed and marginalised peoples.

Christian Nationalism

Nationalism is the understanding that people can be divided into mutually distinct cultural groups defined by shared language, religion, ethnicity, and culture. It believes that these groups should each have their own nations with their own governments that uphold each group's identity. In the United States, Christian nationalism believes that the nation is defined by Christianity and that the government should take active steps to reinforce it. It asserts that the United States must remain a 'Christian nation' and Christianity should be a privileged position in the public sphere.

Christian nationalism can be problematic as cultural identities are elusive. To base political legitimacy on cultural likeness means the political order will be illegitimate to some groups. This can be dangerous in efforts to define who is part of the nation and who is excluded. Many minorities are not included and are then viewed as second-class citizens. Christian nationalism is held mostly by white Americans and therefore creates a racial divide. Christian nationalism distorts the good news as it tries to portray Christ for a worldly political agenda as if it is the only political agenda for every believer. Sometimes Christian nationalism ends up calling evil good and vice versa. It distorts Jesus for a political program and uses the gospel as political propaganda, making the church a tool of the state.[4]

[4] Paul D. Miller, 'What is Christian Nationalism?' *Christianity Today*, February 3, 2021, https://www.christianitytoday.com/ct/2021/february-web-only/what-is-christian-nationalism.html (accessed July 2, 2021).

Christianity needs to unpack and unlearn white colonial Christianity. Christianity does not belong to the United States only, nor does it belong to any one class, race, or ethnicity. Despite Jesus being portrayed as white by white European artists, he was a brown-skinned Palestinian and this must be remembered to stop white nationalism from taking a hold on the United States or other white nations.

Christian nationalism uses the phrase 'religious liberty' to reinforce white cisgender male supremacy. Efforts to include beliefs and practices that challenge that supremacy are framed as 'threats' against religious liberty. Normalising such 'threats' against religious liberty gives whites fuel to legitimise their superiority over people of color. The power to name controls the object being named. For example, parents name their child and thus have power over them when they are young. When it comes to Christianity, naming is important as it can justify a white Christian nationalist social structure that perpetuates and protects white supremacy.[5] Christian nationalism does not want to recognise that we live in a society created by Indigenous genocide and African enslavement. White Christianity preached that white is best and people of color are inferior, which led to a sense of exceptionalism central to Christian nationalism.[6] Thus, white Christianity perpetuates white supremacy. Christian nationalism is problematic to people of color, and we need to do everything that we can to uproot it. Rejecting Christian nationalism does not reject Christianity as they are not the same thing. Rather, it is the Eurocentric lenses, framework, and perspective by which Christianity is seen, projected, and defined that must be eliminated[7]. People of color need to develop Christianity from our own experiences of being disenfranchised, marginalised, and

[5] Miguel De LaTorre, *Decolonizing Christianity: Becoming Bad Ass Believers* (Grand Rapids: Eerdmans, 2021), 58.

[6] Miguel De LaTorre, *Decolonizing Christianity: Becoming Bad Ass Believers* (Grand Rapids: Eerdmans, 2021), 150.

[7] Miguel De LaTorre, *Decolonizing Christianity: Becoming Bad Ass Believers* (Grand Rapids: Eerdmans, 2021), 156, 157.

oppressed. We cannot accept the oppressive white Christian nationalism as true Christianity as that is not the good news that Jesus proclaimed, preached, and lived.

Christian nationalism destroys not only communities of color but also white communities. The violence of white bodies toward people of color is passed down as trauma in generations of white bodies. It is a sin that must be atoned. It will continue to have negative effects until we change our understanding of Christianity as the good news for everyone and proclaim the liberative message found in scripture. Whites achieved power, profit, and privilege in colonial lands through oppressing people of color. Christian nationalism believes that a just society must be created according to a plan controlled by and within their oversight. They do not understand how their societal positions result from institutionalised violence against people of color.

Christian nationalism created political structures that take the lives of people of color. To continue this institutional violence, whites keep telling people of color that they can seek liberation through peaceful and appropriate means.[8] But too often, peaceful means of seeking liberation by people of color are invalidated by white individuals and the white power structure. In other instances, peaceful means turn violent in response to repression. When they do, people of color are villainised. This is a mechanism of controlling people of color and maintaining the status quo so that white people maintain their power and domination.

Christian nationalism and white supremacy have done more damage to people of color around the world than anything else. They have maintained white superiority over people of color and colonised lands, religions, and minds. They are oppressive systems that destroy the lives of people of color and maintain their subordination and marginalisation. White Christian nationalism is not Christianity.

[8] Miguel De La Torre, *Decolonizing Christianity: Becoming Bad Ass Believers*, (Grand Rapids: Eerdmans, 2021), 207.

Differentiation is important so that people of color can embrace Christianity without living in an oppressive social structure that diminishes them and claims their lives.

Sexism

If I first experienced racism in the outside world, I first experienced sexism inside my home, Korean community, and the Korean church. Patriarchy is a part of Confucianism, which is a strong part of Asian culture. Confucianism prefers men, and it was clear that women are second class and subordinate to men. Confucianism desires sons over daughters as the sons will carry on the family line while daughters become part of their husband's family. This patriarchy transferred to the North American context in Asian immigration, including Asian Christianity and the church.

Confucianism taught girls to obey their fathers, married women to obey their husbands, and widows to obey their sons. The clear evidence of male leadership, women's obedience to male leaders, and women's nurturing role in the church cannot be disputed. This patriarchy can be clearly seen in the life of Asian immigrants who attend churches and Asian community events.

Growing up in a patriarchal Asian household and Korean North American church, I saw who had power. At home, it was non-debatable that my sister and I had to obey my father. He was the one with authority and ruled the house as he felt fit. As he was the only male in the house, we all had to obey whatever he said inside and outside. My father wanted complete obedience without any questions or debate, including from my mother.

Sexism was also evident in the Korean church as traditionally only men were elected elders and deacons. The ministers were always men and those who served them, particularly the women, were to act in subservient ways. The women of the church, including my own mother, spent most of their time in the kitchen, making coffee, preparing meals, doing the dishes, and cleaning. The kitchen was the only place for women to 'be', and to serve God and the church.

To my traditional mother, the church kitchen felt like the right place to be since she felt uneasy around the minister and other male leaders of the church. She was timid by nature and around male authority figures at church she felt a need to show her submissiveness, humility, and obedience. I always felt that my mother was doing the same thing at church as at home and felt that she should not be working in the church kitchen. It was always my hope that my mother would gain a sense of her own gifts of leading and teaching and do more in the church than cook and serve.

My family was the only thing I knew, and therefore I assumed that every household was like this. Little did I know that I was wrong. I was wrong and therefore, it was necessary for me to challenge this patriarchal system which was so oppressive to my sister, my mother, and me. An alternative world without patriarchy can exist and it is possible to create that world.

The history of patriarchy in the church needs to be challenged if the church is to be a liberative place for everyone. Just because it is part of the tradition of the church does not mean we need to keep it. We need to challenge it and work towards equality. Just as we cannot accept racism as part of the church and Christianity, we cannot accept sexism. We must be able to overcome the social injustices of racism and sexism so that we can build a more just world.

Conclusion

Fighting racism and sexism is a spiritual fight as much of this is rooted in our understandings of white Christianity, Christian nationalism, and patriarchy. One possible way to fight sexism and racism is to move away from portraying God as a white male and move towards an understanding of Spirit God. The next chapter will look at hybridity and hybrid theology, which can lead to a liberative understanding of God for all humanity.

2

Hybrid Theology

Asian Diaspora

Asians have migrated to all parts of the world, including, from as early as the 1500s, to North America. As Asians migrated, they brought their languages, culture, history, and religion. When Asians migrated to North America, their Asian culture intermixed with the local western culture and impacted how they lived, thought, and practised their faith.

The intermixing of ideas and practices also happened to Christianity. As Christianity spread throughout Europe, Christianity was influenced by philosophy, local concepts, and local practices (Western European liturgy was Latin, Eastern liturgy was Greek). Many Asian immigrants converted to Christianity and adopted Christian lifestyles in their new country. However, as Asians began to suffer due to negative forces such as racism and xenophobia, they started to question their Christianity and recognise the importance of making theology their own. As Asians in the diaspora tried to make sense of their spirituality and their faith amid racism, xenophobia, marginalisation, and discrimination, they could draw on their experiences and understanding of their Asian heritage to construct a theology that makes sense for Asians and for Asians in the diaspora. It is necessary to draw from Asian heritage, religion, and culture to develop a liberative theology that empowers Asians in the diaspora who are struggling with racism, discrimination, and marginalisation. We are created to flourish and become whole. If a theology does not do this but rather destroys one's being, then it needs to be eliminated.

As Asians immigrate around the world, they need to embrace their heritage and not be ashamed of it. Asians should not be embarrassed by their history, culture, or religious heritages, but be proud of their rich history, philosophy, and heritage.

To draw from their Asian heritage and

incorporate key concepts and thoughts into theology will enrich the dialogue and discourse and construct a meaningful and liberative theology. Therefore, it is important to construct theology using elements from both the Asian culture and the western culture to develop a liberative theology that does not feed racism, discrimination, or xenophobia.

Colonialism

Western countries have colonised many countries around the world including parts of Asia. Britain went to India and Malaysia, the United States went to Korea, Spain went to the Philippines, South America, and Africa, and France went to Vietnam, Laos, and Cambodia. They colonised and dominated these Asian countries for their own economic profit and growth. The list of Asian colonialism goes on, and we need to recognise how the western world felt superior and dominant to the East.

Colonialism has many negative effects, such as marginalising native languages, destruction of religious and cultural history, and shame of ethnic identity. Many of the colonised countries had to speak European languages, welcome white culture, and practise white Christianity. Asian countries were told how barbaric their own cultural history was and were taught the superiority of white culture and white Christianity. For example, missionaries who came to Korea pointed out that Shamanism was evil and called it devil worship. They tried to destroy our long tradition of religious practices and spirituality by calling it evil, and they introduced white Christianity. Asians who viewed whites as intelligent and advanced in technology embraced white Christianity. This welcoming of Christianity reinforced the superiority of European philosophy and technology and the destruction of Asian religious teaching, practices, and spirituality.

Under colonialism, white missionaries preached to Asians that superiority of whites was 'good news' and better for Asians. Since whites were the smartest, brightest, and most advanced people in the world, Asians should aspire to become like Europeans in every way possible. They claimed Asians needed to embrace European values if they were going to become a developed country and respected by the rest of the world. They taught white Christianity as if it were the only truth and only gospel. Since Asians were deeply indoctrinated that European culture was good, they welcomed its Christianity without challenging it or comprehending that Christianity is not limited to Latin or Greek or Hebrew texts.

Decolonise

Asia has been colonised by the western world for too long. The western world negated Asian culture, heritage, and religion and instilled in Asia that white is best. Colonisation of not only Asian land and resources, but also of the mind, culture, and religious practices has damaged Asians. As Asians recognise the importance of recultivating and retrieving their own culture and heritage, they decolonise themselves from western ideology, philosophy, religion, and culture. Decolonisation needs to happen in the mind and how we view the world and Christianity.

Christianity was brought over to Asia as a white and pristine religion that was never affected by other religions or cultures. However, Christianity is neither white nor pristine, and it never was. Christianity emerged in the Middle East, and Jesus was a Palestinian Jew, not the white European man that white Christians transformed him into. Christianity, like other major world religions, is a mix of cultural concepts, ideas, and practices. Christianity has been influenced by western culture, philosophy, religion, and even paganism. We see evidence of paganism as we celebrate Easter, which began as a pagan festival to celebrate spring in the northern hemisphere long before the birth of Christianity. As Christianity emerged, this pagan festival became associated with the resurrection of Jesus. This pagan root and practice should be acknowledged in European Christianity so that people realise that Christianity has been syncretistic from the beginning.

The power of whiteness is when

white European cultural aspects mix with Christianity, it appears normal and right to the world while African, Asian, or South American's influence upon Christianity appears evil and syncretistic. For example, Easter was a pagan practice which was brought into Christian practice and became normalised as 'Christian.'

Decolonising our minds is a crucial step towards embracing our authentic selves. It involves retrieving our Asian culture, heritage, and history to make sense of immigrant life, Christianity, and our present context. Decolonising our minds means accepting the hybridity of cultures and religions that occurs within Christianity.

Hybridity

Postcolonial theology embraces hybridity as a tool to decolonise ourselves from western philosophy, ideology, and religion. Hybridity moves towards a liberative way of understanding ourselves and doing theology. The word hybrid has biological and botanical origins. In Latin, the word hybrid means the offspring of a tame sow and a wild boar. A hybrid can be defined as a mongrel or mule, an animal or plant, produced from the mixture of two species.[9] Hybridisation is a mixing of two things while maintaining separation. Hybridisation occurs in all aspects of life as things are not homogenous but heterogenous, discontinuous, and revolutionary.

Hybridity makes difference into sameness and sameness into difference, but in a way that makes the same no longer the same and the different no longer simply different.[10] Hybridity displays the necessary deformation and displacement of all sites of discrimination and domination. It unsettles the demands of colonial power but replicates its identifications in strategies of subversion that turn the gaze of the discriminated back upon the eye of power. Hybrid is the articulation of the ambivalent

[9] Robert J. C. Young, *Colonial Desire: Hybridity in Theory, Culture and Race* (London: Routledge, 1995), 6, 9.
[10] Robert J. C. Young, *Colonial Desire: Hybridity in Theory, Culture and Race* (London: Routledge, 1995), 26.

space where the rite of power is enacted on the site of desire.[11]

Hybridity challenges authority and becomes a form of resistance as it dispenses with dualistic and hierarchical constructions of cultures. Cultures are not static but grow and are dependent on borrowing from each other.[12] Nothing is pure, and the false notion of a pristine western culture needs to be eliminated. Things are always in flux, and we must recognise and accept this.

Hybridity generally refers to the destabilising colonised culture. Within the metropolis, multicultural celebrations of 'cultural diversity' conveniently disguise more serious economic and political disparities.[13] Multiculturalism states that there are multiple cultures. But the reality is that when cultures

[11] Homi Bhabha, *The Location of Culture* (London: Routledge, 1994), 112.

[12] Musa W. Dube, *Postcolonial Feminist Interpretation of the Bible* (St. Louis: Chalice Press, 2000), 51.

[13] Leela Gandhi, *Postcolonial Theory: A Critical Introduction* (New York: Columbia University Press, 1998), 136.

come together, they collide, mix, integrate, synthesise, and recultivate themselves. Postcolonial society is not merely a multicultural society, but a hybrid society. With hybridity, a new product emerges. It is not just a mosaic of cultures existing next to each other, but there is an intermingling of societies. Each culture mixes with other cultures to produce distinct cultures that are different from the original. In hybridity, something changes within society.

Hybridity is ambivalent. Hybridity reverses the formal process of disavowal so that the violent dislocation of colonisation becomes the conditionality of colonial discourse. Hybridity intervenes in the exercise of authority to represent the unpredictability of its presence.[14]

Hybridity embraces both anti-colonial and anti-essentialist strategies in confronting and challenging established hegemony. It is common for the marginalised people to be perceived as 'others' and to develop a 'double consciousness' in the process of

[14] Homi Bhabha, *The Location of Culture* (London: Routledge, 1994), 114.

cultural hybridisation.[15] Hybridity becomes a necessary tool to fight against colonialism and domination. It destabilises the status quo and seeks to fight against the dominating powers which restrict and marginalise the dominated.

Hybrid Identity

As a child of immigrants, I exist between two cultures: Asian, and the dominant, white culture of Europe and North America. Living in between brings forth a hybrid identity as the two cultures mix and form new cultures. It also conjurs up feelings of not belonging in the old culture or in the new culture. Thus, one lives in between cultures and a new, bicultural or hybrid identity emerges. This new identity is a hybrid where two cultures mix and form a new identity. This hybrid identity embraces both cultures and syncretism occurs.

I was born Asian and there is nothing I can do to escape my Asian roots as it is physically evident. I tried to escape my Asian heritage and

[15]   Huey-li Li, 'From Alterity to Hybridity: A Query of Double Consciousness' in *Philosophy of Education*, 2002, 138.

culture for the first 25 years of my life. I despised the patriarchy of my Asian culture which tried to limit my dreams and goals for my life. I despised the physical attributes of my Asianness which led to so much racism and discrimination during my childhood and teenage years. I even disliked the Korean language which was complicated as it has so many ways of addressing people. One speaks to a child, a friend, and to an older adult in different ways with different honorific endings. I resented the 'forced' respect expected to my elders, and it slowly became a source of agony and pain. I felt that an older adult needed to gain my respect and not demand it. As a child, I hated Korean language school because it did not feel worthwhile.

But as I got married and had children of my own, things started to change. The things that I despised about my parents soon became the source of my own child rearing behaviors. For example, I really hated speaking Korean at home, but that is exactly what I ended up doing with my own children until they began elementary school. I also dragged them 'kicking and screaming' to

Korean language school to learn about Korean culture, history, and language.

As a mother of three children, things have come full circle and I have now come to appreciate my Asian heritage. I view my hybrid identity as a twice immigrant as a valuable asset. This hybrid identity should not be despised but cherished, welcomed, and embraced.

On one level, no one lives in a monochromatic culture. Cultures clash with other cultures and new cultures and sub-cultures form. We are living in a time of migration due to war, economy, and climate crisis. Refugees and migration will continue since they are caused by so many factors. Throughout history, people have moved and migrated for various reasons such as food shortages, weather, or economy. As people migrate, new subcultures form and new ways of being emerge, which results in hybrid identities.

Similar to botany when seeds are cross-pollinated and a new variety is created, when two or more cultures merge, a new identity is created. This is the creative part of nature which also occurs in society. It is not something to be diminished, but rather to be celebrated.

I was born in Korea but grew up in Canada. These two cultures, Asian and North American, have informed me in many ways. As a child and a teenager, I was ashamed of my Asian culture and heritage, but I have come to appreciate it. Living 'in between' two cultures, can be rewarding in its diversity, yet also challenging. Living in between two cultures can be problematic as one becomes aware of one's hybrid identity. I had to maneuver the English-speaking culture as well as the Asian culture of my immediate family. As a child, I spoke Korean at home and broken English outside the home. I always sensed a hybrid identity, not belonging in either culture or place, and a feeling of being caught in between two places. I did not feel welcomed by my Korean culture as they felt that I was not Korean enough. I was also not accepted by the white North American culture, which could not accept an Asian as a Canadian or as an American.

Living between two cultures creates a new identity, which is at times difficult to accept or comprehend. Inbetweenness becomes a place of difficulty, which produces anxiety, pain, brokenness, and a sense of non-belonging. There is a feeling of loss due to an overwhelming feeling of not belonging anywhere as you only exist in between places. You are neither here nor there, and you exist in a state of limbo.

Rather than seeing identity or culture as a stable, unchanging reality, it's important to celebrate the changes and fluidity that have always happened throughout history. Hybridity reveals one identity's liminality, instability, impurity, movement, and fluidity. Hybridity is not the dissolution of differences but renegotiates the structure of power built on differences. It is not synonymous with assimilation as assimilation is what the colonialists advocated. It is a two-way process and both parties become interactive so that something new is created.[16] No one's identity is stable because hybridity has created a new human being.

[16] R.S. Sugirtharajah, *Asian Biblical Hermeneutics and Postcolonialism: Contesting the Interpretations* (Maryknoll: Orbis Books, 1998), 125, 126.

Hyphenated Reality

The formation of hyphenated, fractured, multiplied identities occurs for many immigrants and people of color. Any attempt by the 'natives' to redraw their identity by fusing indigenous and imported values was labeled syncretistic and dismissed as a disruptive and negative task. These criticisms are based on Western Christian exclusivity and expansionist perspectives. Hybridity is a wider and more complex web of cultural negotiation and interaction which is forged by redeploying the local and the imported elements. Hybridity is not about melting away differences between 'us' and 'them' but involves a creation, achieved by rejecting imperial attachments and by working through them.[17]

Ethnic minority groups, such as Asian Americans, have been perceived as 'a problem' at work, school, and in the wider society. They are often scapegoated when something goes wrong.

[17] R.S. Sugirtharajah, *Asian Biblical Hermeneutics and Postcolonialism: Contesting the Interpretations* (Maryknoll: Orbis Books, 1998), 16.

When the Covid pandemic occurred, Asian Americans and Asians around the globe were targeted for hate crimes and accused of creating and carrying the virus. There are examples throughout history of ethnic minority groups being targeted, ostracised, and murdered.

The perception of minorities as 'a problem' is a deliberate effort to justify racial oppression in the United States,[18] which is part of the blame game that white Americans play against people of color. Asian Americans and other people of color have never been the 'problem' or the cause of the 'problem'. White settlers, who stole the land from Native Americans and enslaved Africans, created many of the problems that we face today. This is the imperialist's problem, and people of color should not be blamed. Hence rather than viewing ethnic minorities as a problem, we need to celebrate the diversity.

The challenge in having a hyphenated

[18] Huey-li Li, 'From Alterity to Hybridity: A Query of Double Consciousness' in *Philosophy of Education*, 2002, 139.

reality is in the hyphen itself: Asian-American, the realm of in-between where predetermined rules cannot fully apply.[19] The dilemma of the in-between realm is the predicament and the potency of the hyphen. The hyphenated condition does not limit itself to a duality between two cultural heritages. It leads to an active 'search of our mother's garden' (Alice Walker), the consciousness of 'root values' or of a certain Asianness. The hyphen creates a new reality as hybridity occurs and new identities and realities emerge.

Furthermore, the hyphenated reality provides a heightened awareness of other 'minority' sensitivities, such as Third World solidarity and the need for new alliances. The multidimensional desire to be both here and there implies a more radical ability to move between frontiers and cut across ethnic allegiances while assuming a specific and contingent legacy. Changes are implied in the process of restoring the cultural lineage,

[19] Trinh T. Minh-ha, *When the Moon Waxes Red* (New York: Routledge, 1991), 157.

which combines the lore of the past with the lore of the complex present in its histories of immigrations. As soon as we learn to be 'Asians in America', we also recognise that we cannot simply be Asians any longer.[20] Therefore, it gets confusing for Asian Americans who are trying to understand themselves as well as their ongoing changes in culture.

God and Hybrid Context

Knowing ourselves and our context helps us understand God in our midst. God the creator is present within God's creation. God is not distant, but right here with us. God was with the Israelites during their exile and slavery, and God eventually brought them out of Egypt. God was with the lepers, the Samaritan women at the well, Paul in the New Testament, and God helped people in times of trouble. God does not abandon us, but is still present with us today.

We know God through our daily experiences since God is in all aspects of

[20] Trinh T. Minh-ha, *When the Moon Waxes Red* (New York: Routledge, 1991), 159, 160.

our lives. Thus, theology is biography and biography is theology. This is to say that we come to know and understand God through our personal daily experiences. God is not far away, but is present in our lives and we should acknowledge God's presence in our lives. Our love for God expands in our day to day encounter with God. We come to appreciate the fullness of God in our lives as we come to understand God in our lives.

As a theologian, I have come to embrace my Asian identity, culture, and religion in my personal theological journey. In my first book, *The Grace of Sophia,* I examined biblical wisdom and Christology by researching Buddhism, Shamanism, and Confucianism as practiced in Asia. I found many similarities between the concept of wisdom found in the Bible and those found in the holy texts and practices mentioned above. Certainly, there are doctrinal differences among world religions, but there are also striking similarities which draw us in for further examination. Since my first book, I have continued to explore, welcome, and integrate

Asian culture, history, language, concepts, and religion into my own constructive theology to make it comprehensible to me and my community. Hybridity does not damage European Christianity as white people may believe as it only deepens and strengthens Christianity. Christianity has never been pure or pristine as it was always practised in a particular context and culture which always affected Christianity.

Some may find this hybridity or mixing of Asian culture with Christianity alarming and become fearful of syncretism. However, there is not just one theology, but many theologies as theology is intertwined with one's context and culture. When we discuss the doctrine of Trinity, it can be viewed as a form of hybridity, as the three dimensions of God are brought together as one. We celebrate hybridity not only in ourselves, and in theology, but also in how we come to understand and experience God in our daily lives.

Further, if we examine the history of Christian theology for the past two thousand years, we know that white European Christian theologians have been drawing from their culture throughout Christian history. Anselm used his European context of the feudal system in his theory of Atonement. Augustine, who struggled with his own sins, integrated that into his theological exploration of humanity, sin, and the doctrine of humanity. Calvin was an educated lawyer and brought legal thinking and perceiving into writing *Institutes,* which sounds like a law book. We see this repeatedly throughout Christian history.

Theology has always had different forms of syncretism, inculturation and interculturation. Since no theology is done in isolation, it is important to stress this mixing of two things. It has been part of Christian history and will continue to be part of Christianity and Christian practice. Therefore, if we accept white male European theologians to draw from their own culture and context, it should be absolutely acceptable to have a Korean immigrant woman use her culture to do theology.

As we gain insight from postcolonial studies and literature, we can use and adapt the concept of hybridity into theological discourse. We live in a world where people are not in homogenous communities but rather in diverse cultures, and interculturation happens. There is not one culture in society, but many cultures and these cultures become intertwined and interrelated. The term hybrid can be borrowed from science and postcolonial literature to help describe our present reality and help articulate a new theology.

Hybrid Theology

Understanding our reality and how hybridity is part of our context helps us articulate a theology which emerges from our experiences of hybridity. Hybrid theology is mixing of two things and tries to bring both things together and fuses but also maintains separation. It can be a coming together of two (or more) religions, two cultures, and two societies. In the context of Asian Americans, it is a coming together of Christianity and Shamanism, which is the indigenous religion of Korea, and fusing them together to create a new way of worshiping and a new faith. While fusing together, the two religions still maintain separation and their distinct religious identities. This is also a mixing of two cultures, Asian and North American, which influences religious practices and ways of being. These two cultures are very different and thus Asian Americans living in the diaspora feel caught living between two cultures as they try to maintain the distinction between them. Decolonising includes a willingness to embrace and confront indigenous religious and cultural worldviews. Postcolonial thinkers must confront oppressive aspects in one's own indigenous systems. Since no culture is negative or wholly pure, room should always be made for reinterpreting the old, promoting the good, and imagining the new in the hybrid spaces of the native culture.[21] Similarly, hybrid theology tries to reinterpret the old traditions and religions and retrieves what is liberative. Hybrid theology promotes what is good and reimagines hybrid

[21]   Musa W. Dube, 'Postcoloniality, Feminist Spaces and Religion' in *Postcolonialism, Feminism and Religious Discourse*, p. 100-120, ed. Laura E. Donaldson & Kwok Pui Lan (New York: Routledge, 2002), 115, 116.

spaces, which gives life. Hybrid theology welcomes diverse voices and perspectives which can challenge white theology.

Hybrid theology embraces the indigenous religions of hyphenated peoples and syncretises them with Christianity. Thus, for Asian Americans it is a very charismatic Christianity. As we develop hybrid theology, we need to be able to take from the colonised as well as the coloniser and use it to our benefit. Therefore, Christianity and indigenous religions are thus not seen as competing opposites, but as mutual traditions that enrich each other. In so doing, hybridity becomes a decolonising strategy.[22] Hybrid theology shows the struggle that people in the diaspora are experiencing. They need to embrace both religions so that they will experience healing, liberation, and empowerment. Hybrid theology removes the walls between the center and periphery, and other binaries, to work towards equality.

[22] Musa W. Dube, 'Postcoloniality, Feminist Spaces and Religion' in *Postcolonialism, Feminism and Religious Discourse*, p. 100-120, ed. Laura E. Donaldson & Kwok Pui Lan (New York: Routledge, 2002), 117.

Hybrid theology takes into consideration the importance of two societies, two cultures, and two religions. There are numerous differences in values, beliefs, and philosophies between eastern and western societies. These differences can mix and fuse together to create hybridity, which is viable for Asian North Americans to survive and thrive in their new context.

Hybridity becomes the form of cultural difference itself. It challenges the centered, dominant cultural norms with their unsettling perplexities generated out of their 'disjunctive, liminal space'.[23] Similarly, hybrid theology challenges the centered, dominant white theology and reexamines traditional theology which is limiting, damaging, and suffocating for Asian Americans and other people of color. Dominant white theology holds power and dominance which allows it to hold power and appear to be the 'true and only' theology. Other theologies from people of color appear wrong and syncretistic. However, we need to change

[23]   Edward Said, *Culture and Imperialism*, 406; Homi Bhabha, 'DissemiNation' in Bhabha, *Nation and Narration*, 312.

the framework of this approach to Christianity and theology. We need to rethink and reexamine dominant white theology and recognise who developed it and why: to maintain their power. We need to accept this reality and seek new methods of doing theology that break away from whiteness and move towards hybridity and liberation. We need to develop a liberative theology for all people.

Hybrid theology works in two ways. First, it organically creates new spaces and hegemonises structures and scenes, which is positive for people of color who need new spaces to survive. In addition, hybridity intentionally intervenes as a form of subversion, translation, and transformation[24] to create new ways of being. This is also what hybrid theology does within Christianity as it creates new spaces from which one can recognise one's position and dismantle destructive theologies which promote racism, discrimination, and xenophobia. Hybrid theology creates a much-needed space to articulate one's

[24]   Robert J.C. Young, *Colonial Desire: Hybridity in Theory, Culture and Race* (London: Routledge, 1995), 25.

experiences, struggles, and joys so that theology can address such problems and work towards resolutions. Hybrid theology transforms how one does theology and brings praxis into our theology. Hybrid theology offers a liberative, new space to articulate and communicate, and a site for creativity and empowerment where disenfranchised people can achieve freedom from destructive powers.

Conclusion

Hybrid theology is not only for Asian Americans but all who feel caught between binaries which lock them into a vise. The Asian concept of Chi is like the Christian notion of the Holy Spirit. Theology is syncretistic and can adapt its message to the time. A Spirit-Chi pneumatological understanding is not only helpful to Asians wherever they may live but to everyone. Theology helps us understand ourselves and God, which should be liberative and empowering. We should not be destructive towards ourselves and others but focused on love and liberation.

3

Spirit-Chi
Theology

Presbyterian and Spirit

I'M PRESBYTERIAN, SO people often ask me why I study the Spirit. To the world, Presbyterians appear to be one of 'non-spiritual' denominations who are staunch in their ways, rigid, and non-charismatic. Presbyterians are known for strict worship services and doing things 'decently and in good order.' This sounds removed from the Spirit-filled Pentecostals who love the joy of being filled with the Spirit and spontaneous worship.

So how does an ordained Presbyterian minister become involved and immersed in the Spirit? Since God is present everywhere, being filled with the Spirit should come naturally for any Christian because it comes to all of us. The Spirit manifests itself in our lives and bodies in many ways around the world. The Spirit comes in many forms, not just the way experienced by

71

Pentecostals. The Spirit is who the Spirit is and who the Spirit will be (Exodus 3:14) and human beings do not have control over the movement, manifestation, and form of the Spirit.

The Spirit does not just come into our lives in a spontaneous event but can be manifested in various serene ways. The Spirit is within us, in our bodies. We are connected to God through the Spirit which dwells on the earth and fills the universe. That is why different denominations should focus on the Spirit and live in the various manifestations of the Spirit that they encounter in their lives.

My first book is called *The Grace of Sophia* and is a feminist wisdom Christology that centered on Jesus as Sophia Christ. I was excited to reimagine Jesus as the feminine wisdom figure to counter the patriarchal understanding of the divine. I planned to write many books on Sophia Jesus, but that dream turned to the Spirit as I started to teach students of different faith traditions. As I searched for ways to communicate with others of different faith traditions and spiritualities, it became evident that there were so many similarities rather than differences among the world religions. The big similarity was how the different world religions have a similar concept of the Spirit.

My research on Sophia Jesus started my theological journey of trying to understand the divine in feminine terms. Sophia Jesus was also a way for me to engage in interfaith dialogue that is welcoming of one another and not hateful toward anyone. Through my research, it became apparent that the concept of Sophia or wisdom is found in most world religions. However, wisdom does not hold a clear association with the divine in all faiths as the Spirit does. Spirit is more recognisable and more frequently associated with the divine in the major world religions. Since the concept of the Spirit is found and present in most religions, it provides common ground to engage in flourishing interfaith dialogue. As we live in a world where cultures and religions clash with one another, it is important to welcome, dialogue, and embrace people of other faiths. The concept of Spirit is a welcoming entry point of discourse which will pave the way for further dialogue, acceptance, and love for one another. As a result, I never wrote another book on Sophia Christology. Instead, I began writing on the Spirit and the majority of my twenty published books are focused on the Spirit.

Traditional Spirit

The traditional notion of Spirit was understood through the German term *Geist*. Christian theologians were prominent in Europe, so when German theologians began to influence theological discourse by writing theology in German, they used the term *Geist* to talk about the Spirit. *Geist* conveyed a philosophical understanding of the Spirit. It is translated as ghost, spirit, mind, and intellect. It is also a masculine gendered word, which reinforces the patriarchal notions of the divine. It was viewed as a Spirit out there in space and not as a Spirit within all of us. *Geist* neither conveys a Spirit that is close nor a Spirit that draws us closer to the divine. *Geist* commonly appears in German philosophy, especially that of Hegel. This notion of the Spirit impacted western Christian understanding of the Spirit for much of Christian history. This western understanding of the Spirit is restrictive for Asian Americans who have had a similar but more expansive understanding of the Spirit.

Chi

Asian Americans live in hybridity and understand their lives to be hybrid. Thus, it is understandable to have a hybrid perspective of the Spirit. To move towards a hybrid understanding of the Spirit, we begin by recognising the rich history, religious traditions, and cultures from Asia. There is a wealth of language and concepts in Asia which can widen our understanding of Christian liberative theology. We should not restrict ourselves to just one way of thinking, speaking, and imagining, but be open to all available ways of conceiving God and how we come to understand God in our lives. The more languages, words, and concepts that we have to help us understand God, the deeper we will come to know God, the infinite Creator. Our finite minds and our limited languages can never comprehend the fullness and infiniteness of God.[25] But we do not give up; we try our best to understand and come to a deeper sense of who God is.

One key concept I draw from my Asian heritage is Chi to help develop a liberative pneumatology and a hybrid theology. Chi is translated as wind, energy, spirit, and breath which is similar to the Old Testament *ruach* and New Testament *pneuma.* There are approximately 65,000 languages in the world and it's important to decenter the English language

[25] 'Let man then contemplate the whole of nature in her full and grand majesty, and turn his vision from the low objects which surround him. Let him gaze on that brilliant light, set like an eternal lamp to illumine the universe; let the earth appear to him a point in comparison with the vast circle described by the sun; and let him wonder at the fact that this vast circle is itself but a very fine point in comparison with that described by the stars in their revolution round the firmament. But if our view be arrested there, let our imagination pass beyond; it will sooner exhaust the power of conception.' Pascal, Blaise. *Pensées - Enhanced Version*, Christian Classics Ethereal Library. Kindle Edition. Paragraph 72.

to help decolonise us from the western world. Some ideas and concepts are better captured in some languages than others and some languages have various meaningful and helpful concepts that may not be present in the English language. For example, the Korean language is emotional as Koreans carry a lot of emotions and pain with them. Some of the pain is so deep and heavy that many Koreans feel that they will carry it with them to their death and even into their afterlife. Thus there are multiple words such as *han* and *han-pu-ri* to express deep sorrows and pain. *Han* is a difficult word to translate into the English language as it embodies a deep unjust suffering which is experienced by individuals, communities and even Korea as a country as Korea has been invaded and colonised by other countries. *Han* embodies and conveys the immense pain of unjust suffering due to unjust systems which are set up to create deep distress and agony. Thus, different languages help us in our theological language and discourse as it widens our lens and deepens our theological thinking. It ultimately helps us

77

in our theological task of liberation.

Chi is an important and familiar concept in Asia. It is part of the everyday language for Asians. For example, in Korea, people may greet you with, 'How is your Chi today?' If your Chi is low, friends will try to cheer you up and try to help build up your Chi. Asians use the word Chi in their day-to-day discourse and living. Chi is found in words such as reiki and Tai Chi where people practice harnessing energy to move the energy flow inside our body.

When Chi is blocked in our body or it cannot flow properly, it can cause health problems to our body and spirit. Chinese doctors were able to map the flow of Chi in the body even before western doctors were able to map the flow of blood in one's body. Chinese doctors knew that the key to being healthy was to have Chi flow through the body without obstruction or blockages. Chi flows in the body to help cure ailments and bodily pain. Traditional Chinese medicine uses acupuncture to help correct the blockage or flow of Chi in one's body. Asians also practice tai chi to help Chi flow correctly in one's body. Chi gives us life.

When someone dies, their Chi leaves their body. Chi is energy and it is what keeps the body warm and hence once Chi leaves the body, the body becomes very cold and lifeless.

Asians had this concept of Chi for thousands of years because it gives life. Some of the ancient Chinese character for Chi was a diagram of a bowl of rice with steam rising on top of it. Chinese and East Asians eat rice almost daily and is the main food staple. Rice is what sustains us and keeps us alive. Rice is crucial for East Asian diet as it is consumed and used in so many ways as rice is used to make rice drinks, rice wine, rice bread, rice cakes, rice cookie, rice glue and rice paper. When we first immigrated to Canada, I remember we didn't have much to eat, but we always had rice at our meals. In Korean, the word for 'meal' is 'rice'. So when people ask, 'have you eaten?', it is quite literally asking 'have you had rice?'. As a child, I remember using rice as glue for my school art projects and school projects as we did not have 'white glue' at home. Therefore, rice is crucial to the life of Asians and in the same way, so is Chi. Chi is like rice as Chi is similarly viewed as something which sustains us and keeps us alive.

Chi reinforces the notion of Spirit as breath, lifegiving and helper in all things. The Spirit is key and important in our ways of thinking and being. We need to be aware of Chi in our lives and see how we can move forward with this concept of life. Furthermore, Chi is an embodied understanding of the Spirit in contrast to the predominantly philosophical way of viewing the Spirit in white western patriarchal theology. In western theology, Spirit is something 'out there', nebulous and not tangible. Spirit is sometimes viewed as hazy, unclear, and uncertain. But in the Asian tradition, Chi is something concrete and more certain. Chi is in our bodies and flows throughout our body, much like blood does. Chi is also all around us in the universe and it is what gives us life and sustains it. Chi is in all living things and is part of the universe. The understanding of Chi in our bodies shows that the Spirit of God lives within us, gives us life, and supports our life.

Spirit-Chi

Since Christianity has been so white and patriarchal for too long, it is overdue to widen its perspective and understanding of Spirit God, which includes the Asian concept of Chi.

Chi is Spirit and for me as an Asian American theologian, it is important to use Asian terms, languages and concepts to understand and help expand and address the traditional western male theology. This is the task of hybrid theology, and we need to embrace it as it works to eliminate biased theologies. Hybrid theology is derived when two different things come together to form a new product. Hybrid theology brings two things together to form a new entity. In hybrid theology, the Asian concept of Chi comes together with the Hebrew *ruach* and Greek *pneuma* to form a deeper and more meaningful understanding of the Spirit. Hybrid theology challenges the status quo and the dominant white center, which is promising and liberative for Asians and Asian Americans who experience racism and discrimination.

The Asian concept of Chi is an embodied understanding which draws us closer to the divine. The Spirit of God is not a nebulous concept out there, but it is within us and gives us life. It is all around us and it is within us. It gives us life and it provides us good ways of living. Without Chi, we will die. In death, Chi, which is the lifegiving Spirit and warmth, leaves our bodies and goes out into the world.

Exploring cultures around the world helps us to articulate a meaningful theology that speaks to diverse people. Hybrid theology does not negate one's experiences, heritage, or culture, but rather embraces them and searches for liberative ways of understanding humanity and the divine. The term Spirit-Chi springs forth from hybrid theology, as it draws from Asian concepts to help us articulate a meaningful theology that is liberative for Asian Americans. Furthermore, hybrid theology fights racism, discrimination, and xenophobia, which is helpful as oppression is destructive of our Chi. We need to build one another's Chi to strengthen and empower each other.

The task of theology is to help us understand more deeply who God is. Theology uses language, words, concepts, and ideas to help us get to a more meaningful comprehension of the divine. However, language is limiting as they are finite tools trying to understand the infinite God. Thus, we must acknowledge language limitations and therefore seek new ways, languages, and concepts to help us draw closer to an understanding of God. When it comes to understanding the divine who is infinite, our finite minds cannot comprehend, describe, or conceive the fullness of God.

Fight Racism

The church exists in society, which must deal with racism, discrimination, and xenophobia. During the COVID pandemic where the incidents of Asian hate rose world-wide, Asian Americans were seeking to construct a liberative theology that will work towards embracing Asians, Asian Americans, people of color around the globe. Hybrid theology fights racism around the world and works toward equality, inclusion, and fairness.

Racism poisons and destroys communities, breaks people's spirits, and even kills. The evils of racism need to be named, and Christianity and theology need to fight against racism. White governments have perpetuated hate towards people of color and created a hierarchy of people with whites at the top and Blacks at the bottom. If Christianity is going to fight racism, we need to eliminate white Christianity. Christianity emerged in the middle east and was not white at the beginning. White supremacy has dominated much of Christianity and created a white, male God which is neither biblical nor Christian. Christianity became a white religion with a white Jesus and a white God. Whiteness was read into the holy scriptures, and Christianity was made white. White supremacy creates a hierarchy of people and maintains the status quo to keep white people at the top. We need to divorce our thinking from white supremacy and work towards a biblical understanding that is more inclusive, liberating, and lifegiving.

If we continue to focus on Christology, a white, male Jesus and whiteness are reinforced in a religion that did not begin white. A hybrid theology and a Spirit centered theology moves us away from a white Christianity and helps us eliminate racism. Spirit theology neither portrays a white God nor a white Jesus, and it does not center whiteness. Rather, Spirit theology focuses on God as Spirit who is neither Black nor white, male nor female, straight, or gay. Spirit theology tries to destroy destructive ideologies like Christian nationalism, white supremacy, colonialism, and heteronormative white male patriarchal theology. Spirit theology decenters Christianity from whiteness and maleness and tries to create a base where all people are welcomed and embraced. Therefore, Spirit theology is liberative and non-destructive. Spirit theology helps us recognise that all are created in God's image and we are all valuable as there is no hierarchy of people and whites are not on the top.

In addition to Spirit theology, a hybrid theology that embraces Spirit-Chi moves us away from the patriarchal white notions of God and toward an understanding beyond anthropomorphism and whiteness. It challenges us to welcome, embrace and accept other cultures and other ways of perceiving the divine to achieve a deeper and fuller understanding of the Christian faith and God. A hybrid theology which recognises that nothing is pristine nor unmixed is appropriate to help us overcome racism and sexism in the church and in our wider society. Hybrid theology reminds us we need to be cognisant of otherness and welcome them into the kin-dom of God.

People of other faiths also have Spirit and perhaps this can bring us together to have a worthwhile, meaningful and flourishing dialogue. As a result, we fight racism and recognise that we are all related, and all created in God's image.

Fighting against Sexism

Not only is there destructive racism in our society, but also sexism that affects more than half of the world's population. Patriarchal societies have subordinated women as second-class citizens. Women are more than half of the church's population. Perpetuating patriarchal doctrines and theology in the church damages our perception of women. Misinterpretations of scripture and patriarchal cultures have maintained the subordination of women in the church. The negative consequences of such a view are sexual abuse of women, physical assault on women, and the continuous second-class role of women in the church. It maintains women in subordinate positions and abuse of women is tolerated, accepted, and perpetuated.

Hybrid theology and Spirit God can help us overcome patriarchy in the church and the masculine understanding of God which perpetuates sexism. We cannot continue to accept sexism as part of the everyday life of the church and how we view God. We cannot blindly view God as male as it consequently makes men feel closer to God since they are created in God's maleness. We need to eliminate patriarchy that we find in society, religion, and culture and reverse the negative effects it has had on us.

Rather than speaking about a male father God that perpetuates a patriarchal God, we need to speak of a Spirit God, which moves us away from the maleness and whiteness of God. A male God perpetuates sexism as men are viewed to be closer to God while as Spirit God is gender neutral and moves us a step closer to eliminating patriarchy within Christianity.

There is gender injustice in this world as patriarchy reigns in most cultures. Women are abused, and verbally and physically assaulted, sometimes killed. Women are paid less than men, and women need to maneuver in the male-dominated world which is not easy to accomplish in certain spheres of society. But if women are to survive and flourish, it is necessary to overcome abuse and subordination. Women are half the world's population and Christianity needs to be in this fight to work towards gender justice. This is crucial for all of us.

Interfaith dialogue

The world is shrinking as it becomes easier to travel globally and travel quickly. People are migrating due to various economic, social, political, and religious reasons. Now with the terrible effects of climate change, climate refugees as well as political refugees are landing on our borders with increasing frequency. As people of different cultures, faith and religious backgrounds live, work, and socialise together, it becomes increasingly important to engage in interfaith dialogue intentionally so we can maintain peace and love our neighbors.

The power of religion should not be ignored. Religions can either build up or tear down neighbors. We need to be able to speak with one another and engage in interfaith work so that we can build one another up rather than tear one down. The power of interfaith dialogue is important and crucial for our time as we live in a migrant world. As one intentionally engages in interfaith work, it is important to find ways of engagement rather than disengagement.

As a woman of Asian heritage, I welcome and embrace the long, rich Asian religious history. In our long history, the introduction of Christianity to the East is more of a recent phenomenon; Asians have been religious and spiritual throughout their history. Asians have always been people of religious faith who have sought the divine to help them, guide them, and heal them. In their rich religious history and tradition, it is important to look at similarities among world religions rather than their differences. Most of the world religions have a concept and word for Spirit. They have different words for Spirit, but they all refer to the life-force, breath, energy, and Spirit of God. This similarity is very important as it becomes an entry way to engage in wonderful interfaith dialogue. Once one finds similarities between religions, it becomes harder to hate one another and easier to embrace the other. Once we see similarities, it makes us wonder if there are that many differences among religions and whether we are all talking about the same God. This is important as the world gets smaller, more migration is occurring, and climate refugees are on the increase, we need to be able to live with one another and recognise the similarities rather than the differences. This is important as we try to live a flourishing life.

Intentional dialogue leads to acceptance, welcome and embrace rather than xenophobia and hatred. Hybrid theology and an understanding of a Spirit God can help us overcome the fear of the other. The different world religions also view Spirit in similar ways as the Asian concept of Chi. This helps bridge the various world religions together to find commonality and move us away from differences. This is helpful and it enriches our understandings of each other and of God.

Peace and Justice

The Spirit of God lives in all of us. It is energy, wind, breath, and vibration which motivates and empowers us to do something for the good of all humanity and all God's creation. The Spirit of God is bountiful and pushes us towards a life of goodness. A life of goodness can be achieved if everyone has equal access to all the things that powerful, white people have. As the Spirit of God resides in us, we recognise that it motivates us to make changes in our world. It is the vibration which pushes us to work for justice. There is so much work to do for racial, gender, and climate justice.

The biggest social justice issue of our time is the climate crisis. Storms are getting worse, overpopulation is affecting creatures, plants, and human beings, and carbon emissions are getting higher. If we don't do anything about this crisis, it will only get worse for the planet, which may destroy the planet. We need to act now before it is too late and beyond repair.

Our doctrine of creation has been weak for much of Christian history. We centered creation around humanity as if everything were created for our use and 'abuse'. We are a small part of God's glorious creation and are called to be good 'stewards' of creation and not selfish destroyers of it.

An understanding of God as Spirit will greatly move us to work towards saving the planet and God's creation to achieve climate justice.

Conclusion

Hybrid theology and Spirit centered theology helps overcome some of the difficulties that we face as immigrants, people of color, and women. Christian theology that perpetuates sexism, racism, and discrimination can no longer be accepted as Christian theology. This should no longer be accepted as the good news. We need to challenge traditions within the church and reimagine ways of understanding God within our own context. As we seek God's presence in the world and in our lives, a Spirit-Chi understanding of God is liberating. A hybrid Spirit-Chi theology helps us overcome some of the shortfalls of white male western theology. It motivates us to work for peace and justice and fight against all forms of injustice in our society.

Conclusion

THIS SHORT BOOK on my theological journey helped me to articulate where I have been, including the pain I experienced growing up, and where I am going. Theology does not stop; it is a continuous journey as one comes to a deeper understanding of God in various stages of one's life.

As I struggled with the maleness of Jesus which reinforced a male God, I was in search of other ways to comprehend God in my life. The Spirit God comforted me and empowered me. The Spirit God allowed us to move away from a male deity visualised by European art. The maleness and whiteness of God legitimised racism and sexism in the church and the wider society.

When I came to appreciate my Korean culture, which happened when my kids were born, I needed to find a way to reconcile it with the culture my family moved to, which were opposites. Once I came to appreciate my

Asian heritage, it became important for me to search my heritage for theological elements.

The popular concept of Chi stuck out to me. It is in the everyday languages of East Asians and in words like reiki, and tai chi. It has a similar understanding of the Hebrew *ruach* and New Testament *pneuma*. It became a converging point for me as the Asian concept of Chi expanded the biblical understanding of Spirit. Chi reinforced very clearly how God is within us, since Chi is an embodied notion of Spirit. God has never left us but is always with us, within us, and moving us with God Spirit. Spirit-Chi forms us, provides for us, sustains us, moves us, and gives us life. We cannot live without Spirit-Chi.

As Christian theology becomes globalised, I hope we can eliminate the traditions of European art and the history of European colonialism, which have been harmful to the native traditions and to colonised people. Christianity at birth was not a white religion. The elimination of whiteness, white privilege, and white supremacy will help us heal the damages of racism and xenophobia. It will help us accept and embrace the other as we realise that the Spirit of God is within all of us.

Spirit-Chi also helps societies and churches overcome sexism and patriarchy. Women have been made second-class citizens as the maleness of Jesus and God were emphasised. Women are also often seen as unclean, as in the Torah, in biblical characters like Raheb, Eve, and the Samaritan woman. In many parts of Asia, women are taught to 'obey' men and this takes away women's autonomy, sense of being, and personhood. If we recognise and embrace Spirit-Chi, we recognise that the maleness of God is sublimated and a focus on the Spirit is emphasised. This helps us move towards a society of gender equality and away from patriarchal Christianity.

My own theological journey has been full of turmoil due to racism and sexism. With our approach to God as Spirit, we overcome these dangerous ways of life and move towards embracing people of color and women, both of whom are important to the body of Christ and to God's creation.